# THE 7 SECRETS

## FOR EFFORTLESS TEAM SUCCESS

SIDDHESH KHATU

Book Title: THE 7 SECRETS FOR EFFORTLESS TEAM SUCCESS

Author name: Siddhesh Khatu

Edition: First Edition

ISBN-13: [Your ISBN-13]

For permissions or inquiries, contact:

Visit www.coneandarc.in for more information.

# Dedication

This book is for everyone finding team leadership tricky, for anyone struggling to lead a great team or make a good team. It is dedicated to making it easier. Let's succeed together!

# Acknowledgments

Thanks to my teachers who taught me to find happiness in simple things during my school days in my hometown. They taught me to understand things over using fancy words, so I'm keeping this book simple.

Thanks to my late father, Mr. Subhash chandra, and my dear mother, Mrs. Sukhada, who were teachers in our small town. They not only grew me up but taught me important life lessons.

I'm grateful to my brothers, Rohan and Rugwed, who not only helped me out financially, but also guided me in my career. Thanks to them, and to my sisters for also showing me love and support.

In my business life, I would like to give a shout-out to my friend, Mr. Viraj Dali. His advice and support have always been invaluable to me.

I want to express my deepest gratitude to my wife eisha. I appreciate your love and the wonderful gifts you have given me in the form of our two daughters. Thank you for supporting me and being my strength.

Lastly, I would like to thank all the other family members and friends who have always believed in me. Your encouragement keeps me going every day.

I owe a lot to my coach, Mitesh Khatri, for inspiring and guiding me while writing this book.

I am also grateful to Dr. Meghna Dixit and Ms. Nayan Agarwal for their invaluable support and guidance.

Their influence has truly transformed my perspective on life, leaving me with a significantly altered mindset.

I want to take this opportunity to express my sincere gratitude to everyone who played an important role in bringing this book to life. It wouldn't have been possible without your contribution and support.

A special thanks to various online coaches for their unwavering encouragement and insightful feedback throughout the writing process. Your feedback helped me shape the final outcome.

This book was possible because of the amazing support I received from my team. Your efforts helped me as well as contributed to the lessons contained in this book.

Lastly, thank you to the readers. Your interest in these strategies and dedication to improving team dynamics made this book possible. Thanks for being part of this journey.

# TABLE OF CONTENTS

# Introduction

When it comes to a one-stop resource for team leadership, "Effortless Team Success" by Siddhesh Khatu is an excellent choice. With more than a decade of experience in business coupled with interior design, Siddhesh has honed the art of building awesome teams that are not only functional but also high-performing and exceed expectations.

It is a book that goes well beyond just being a little bag of tips and tricks. Siddhesh breaks down his secrets of the trade with practicable strategies and anecdotes, so that one can have a blueprint for building winning teams. You will learn key principles that range from building trust to creating accountability and aligning everyone toward the same goal.

What makes "Effortless Team Success" unique is the mentorship of Khatu. Through his words, you will find inspiration and knowledge from the challenges he has encountered and the victories he has celebrated. You can discover how to build trust, make everyone accountable, and direct them all towards the same goals.

At the end of this journey, you will not only lead teams but also see them realize their full potential, leaving behind a legacy of achievement and cooperation. The book is beneficial for both experienced managers who are developing their talents and those who love building high-performance team dynamics. "Effortless Team Success" gives you tips as well as ideas needed for your success.

You can reach Siddhesh Khatu via either of these ways:

#SECRET 1

# CRISP AND CLEAR COMMUNICATION

"Effective communication is one of the most critical aspects that define effective collaboration within a group. I remember it might also be quite obvious, but it is actually a crucial element in the processes of communicating and sharing information, as well as in planning and scheduling events and tasks.

It implies that there is a clear understanding between all members of the working team regarding the tasks assigned and the objectives to be achieved. When messages are organized logically and clearly using straightforward language and with appropriate additional information, communication within a team is more effective, and the probability of mistakes and misinterpretations declines. It also encourages positive team relations where the members of the team feel that they are listened to as well as appreciated. This results in higher morale, productivity, and the overall success of the team.

# THE IMPORTANCE OF EFFECTIVE COMMUNICATION

Here is the marketing team, which analyzes the marketing plan the client needs. In this case, the team needs to develop a marketing strategy to launch a new product smart home hub with the four members described below.

1. Rajesh - (Team Leader)
2. Siddharth - (Content Creator)
3. Pooja - (Graphic Designer)
4. Priya - (Social Media Manager)

Let's take a closer look at how they conducted their marketing campaign meeting for the launch of their new product. They used open dialogue and clear communication to make it easy to understand. The most important information was shared first and sentences were kept short. We'll explain in simple language to make it easy to follow.

**Rajesh** (Team Leader): Hello, all of you. I am grateful you are here. Today, we are going to talk about the upcoming marketing strategy in regard to the new product that is to be released. So, Pooja, could you begin by summarizing the information about the product and its main characteristics?

**Pooja** (Graphic Designer): Well, of course, Rajesh. The new product is a smart home hub device designed to control light and temperature in a home. It is convenient and eco-friendly for users, and its main functions include voice assistants and scheduling.

**Rajesh** (Team Leader): Great, thanks Pooja. Siddharth, what do you think of any concept for presenting the product's features through our content?

**Siddharth** (Content Creator): Yes I think we should start with a blog post highlighting the common issues people face with traditional home systems and how our product solves them. Then, we can create short, engaging social media posts showcasing its key features and benefits.

**Rajesh** (Team Leader): Excellent. Priya, how can we leverage social media to build anticipation?

**Priya** (Social Media Manager): I suggest we create teaser posts with countdowns to the launch, along with some behind-the-scenes content showing the product development process. This will help generate excitement and curiosity among our followers.

**Rajesh** (Team Leader): That sounds like a solid plan. Pooja, do you predict any design challenges or considerations for the campaign visuals?

**Pooja** (Graphic Designer): Yes, one challenge might be effectively visualizing the concept of a "smart home" without making it too technical. I'll focus on using relatable visuals that demonstrate convenience and comfort.

**Rajesh** (Team Leader): Thanks for bringing that up. Siddharth, Pooja's point is crucial. Make sure the content aligns with her design approach to maintain consistency.

**Siddharth** (Content Creator): Got it, Rajesh. Pooja, I'll collaborate closely with you to ensure the content and visuals complement each other seamlessly.

**Rajesh** (Team Leader): Collaboration is key. Now, before we wrap up, let's establish a timeline. Pooja, when do you think you can have the initial design concepts ready?

**Pooja** (Graphic Designer): I can have them ready for review by the end of this week.

**Rajesh** (Team Leader): Perfect. Siddharth, once you have those concepts, please start working on the blog post draft. Priya, begin brainstorming the teaser posts and content ideas based on Priya and siddharth's work.

**Priya** (Social Media Manager): Will do.

**Rajesh** (Team Leader): Fantastic. Let's rejoin in two days to review the initial concepts and align our progress. If anyone encounters any roadblocks, please reach out to me or the relevant team member for assistance. Thank you, everyone. Let's create an outstanding campaign together!

**Team**: Thanks, Rajesh!

In this particular case, it is easy to see how communication was a decisive factor in the team's performance. They were able to accomplish these outlines through speaking, listening, questioning, elaborating, maintaining specific goals, and creating a synergistic environment. I can appreciate that the team leader, Rajesh, recognizes everyone's contribution and ensures that everyone is moving in the right direction. The dedication of the team is also seen through their constant meetings and readiness to help members of the group.

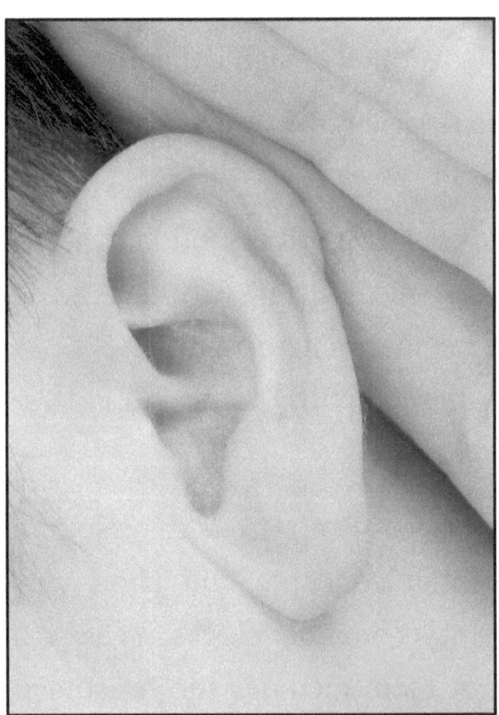

*"Remember, clear and continuous communication will be the backbone of our success."*

*** Unknown***

# 10 STRATEGIES AND PRACTICES TO HAVE EFFECTIVE COMMUNICATION

Here are some strategies and practices to produce effective communication within your team:

I. **Open and Transparent Communication:**

Create an environment where members of the team feel comfortable expressing themselves and come forward with what they want to say, their opinion, their worries, or feedback. Make sure that each person can freely share their ideas with the rest of the group without being judged.

II. **Active Listening:**

Encourage team members to embrace listening as an active process. This includes listening seriously to the other party, coming up with questions concerning the ongoing conversation, and demonstrating concern to the speaker. This practice helps avoid misunderstandings and shows respect.

III. **Regular Team Meetings:**

Many organizational communication difficulties can be solved by having standard check-in meetings to discuss progress, issues, and planned work. These meetings allow updates to be shared, and if any problems are encountered, they are discussed amongst the group.

IV. **Clear Expectations:**

The scope of work should also be well defined, including the responsibilities of team members and their performance expectations. One of the major reasons that leads to poor communication is when individuals do not have clear visions of what is required of them

V. **Use of Technology:**

Take advantage of the available messaging applications, task and project management systems, and virtual meeting apps. These tools enable the exchange of information in a relatively short amount of time and enable collaboration by teleworking.

VI. **Face-to-Face Interaction:**

Whenever possible, try having face-to-face interactions. Face-to-face communication can also foster more personal interdependence and appreciation among members.

VII. **Conflict Resolution Skills:**

Develop strategies and introduce the use of conflict-solving skills among the team members. It is a knowledge that conflict cannot be completely eliminated; thus, ideas on how such conflict can be dealt with in a way that will not demotivate the whole team are needed.

VIII. **Arranging Meetings:**

Arranging a one-on-one session with the members of the team at a particular interval. These meetings provide an opportunity for more personalized communication and addressing individual concerns.

IX. **Encourage Questions:**

Cultivate a culture where team members feel comfortable asking questions. Encouraging curiosity helps uncover potential issues and encourages learning.

X. **Consistent Updates:**

Keep team members informed about project updates, changes, and important decisions. Consistent updates prevent surprises and help maintain trust within the team.

Bear in mind that ensuring successful communication is not a one-time activity but rather a continuous process that presupposes the mutual efforts of the participants. It is imperative to adopt effective communication strategies and promote them within the organizational context so that its members can observe that their colleagues appreciate, value, and pay attention to their ideas in the process of solving common problems.

The rationale for clear and crisp communication, therefore, is to make sure that its purpose is to convey a message in a manner that will be understood with a certain level of precision within the shortest time possible. Sometimes, people prefer to solve problems with more brainstorming or information sharing, while others may want more focus on task orientation.

Therefore, by incorporating efficient communication, others within the team will foster camaraderie, learn to share, and work collectively towards the accomplishment of said objectives. Let us discuss an interior project that got delayed primarily due to a lack of communication, and then how, with the help of strategies and clear communication, the issues were sorted out and the project was successfully completed at the right time.

## Communication Success Stories

This story is about Rahul, who is a project manager in a dynamic interior design studio. The studio has a group of junior and experienced staff of interior designers who are expected to transform a client's office from a dull and deserted area into a lively working space.

Rahul, being energetic, got along well with the project in the beginning, but he faced some issues he did not expect. As the weeks went by, the project faced various setbacks, including major miscommunication between the design and construction teams, which led to differences in the original plans and specifications.

Additionally, there were delays in material deliveries, which further complicated the situation. As a result, the project timeline extended beyond the initial estimates, causing the client's frustration to grow. The budget was also tight due to the delays, and the project team's morale dipped.

So the situation was such that Rahul recognized the need for a correction, and he immediately called for an emergency project review meeting. He aimed to identify the issues and come up with a plan to get the project back on track.

Everybody Gathered around a table, the team discussed the challenges openly, and with lots of discussion, it became clear that we needed to improve communication between the design and construction teams, which was critical. As the project was delayed, finding alternative suppliers for the delayed materials was an essential solution to prevent further delays.

So With reenergized commitment, the team embraced the solution. They established a streamlined communication process, introducing regular status updates and check-ins between the design and construction teams. The project manager, Rahul, also reached out to multiple suppliers to speed up material deliveries. Over the following weeks, the project team worked diligently to implement the solution. The improved communication promoted better coordination, and the revised material sourcing strategy resulted in quicker deliveries.

Finally, the day arrived for the project's completion. The working area was redesigned into a beautiful and productive space that met and maybe even exceeded the client's requirements. The difficulties that arose at the beginning of the project, on the contrary, proved that the team can work effectively when encountering various problems.

In the end, the experience highlighted the significance of **effective communication** and proactive problem-solving in interior projects. The team realized that if we had clear and crisp communication between us before, we would not have faced challenges between the design and construction teams. The team took a lesson from that and will henceforth have open and transparent communication with regular status updates and check-ins between the design and construction teams.

So regular collaboration and quick adjustments were essential to navigate unexpected obstacles and deliver exceptional results.

**So here is an assignment for you that should do with your team for effective communication!**

Various exercises can be used to improve team communication. Here's a simple and effective exercise:

**Activity: Two Truths and One Lie.**

**Objective:** To enhance communication skills, encourage active listening, and build relationships within the team.

**Instructions:**

- **Preparation**: Each team member prepares two true statements and one false statement about themselves (it can be about health, work, fun, behavior, etc)

- **Sharing**: Sit in a circle or arrange a virtual meeting. One by one, each team member shares their three statements, mixing them up to make it challenging.
- **Guessing**: After a person shares their statements, the rest of the team guesses which statement is the false one. The person who shared the statements reveals the lie and explains the truth.

I know sometimes exercises can feel a bit tricky but don't worry. Just take it step by step. Remember, if you ever feel stuck or unsure, don't hesitate to ask for help. It's okay – we're all here to support each other. Communication is the key. If you're not sure about something, just speak up. Remember, the key is to create a safe and respectful environment where team members feel comfortable sharing. The exercise can be adjusted based on the team's preferences and dynamics.

**What are the Benefits you will get after doing this exercise?**

- **Active Listening**: Team members need to listen carefully to the statements and analyze them to make an accurate guess.
- **Communication**: Sharing personal facts encourages open conversation and helps team members get to know each other better.

- **Observation**: Team members observe body language and tone to make better guesses, improving non-verbal communication skills.
- **Engagement**: This activity promotes engagement and participation, cultivating a more comfortable atmosphere for communication.

**Variations you can do :**

- **Two Truths and a Dream**: Instead of a lie, participants share a dream they hope to achieve.
- **Guess the Experience**: Team members share an experience they've had, and others guess whether it was positive or negative.
- **Team Building Twist**: Split the team into smaller groups and have each group present their three statements to the larger team. This adds a team-building competitive element.

I hope you've finished this exercise by now with your Team! If not, no worries - you can do it now, remember "***Your one step can change your life but it is important to take that step and the right time is Now*** ".

Ultimately, a team that masters crisp and clear communication nurtures team connections, productivity, and success.

*"To effectively communicate, we must realize that we are all different in the way we perceive the world and use this understanding as a guide to our communication with others."*

*** Tony Robbins***

**Take a moment to ask the following questions:**

1. Is my message easily understandable by all team members?

   ______________________________________________

   ______________________________________________

2. In my message to teams, have I captured the elements of why, what, and how?

   ______________________________________________

   ______________________________________________

3. How must I personally contribute towards ensuring we develop the culture of listening and practice utmost communication in the team?

___________________________________________

___________________________________________

The thinking of these questions as to how can we understand each other and how can we make this conversation better directs us towards the correct path for improvement in communication. Hence communication is vital since it will allow us to be in a position to relate well with other human beings in our work teams, families, and other forums. Therefore, in an effort to answer these questions, we also learn the craft of speaking and listening, which is a natural interaction between people.

In sum, one of the critical success factors in teams is effective communication. It is now clear that simple and straightforward inter- and intrapersonal communication enables better teamwork. So if all the members of that team understand what the other person is doing or what is happening, that is the best of communication in teams. By listening effectively, providing constructive feedback, and choosing the right media of communication, such as formal meetings or formal e-mails, the right message gets to everyone in the team. If all these easy rules are adhered to and everyone continues to practice them, it makes the team efficient, united, and ready to handle any obstacle that comes their way. That's right—the ability to communicate clearly is like a superpower for all teams!

As you finish reading this chapter, get ready for the next exciting topic: "**Role clarity and effective delegation** ". In the next part, you'll learn about how clear roles in a team and smartly sharing tasks can make working together even better. You'll see how these ideas help everyone work together smoothly and get more work done. Flip the page to find out how these tips can make your teamwork awesome!

# SECRET 02

# ROLE CLARITY AND DELEGATE EFFECTIVELY

“Role clarity and effective delegation are essential aspects of building and managing successful teams. Employees must have to understand their positions in the teams that are being formed and how these positions are going to be delegated. Role definition, on the other hand, is the process by which an individual, a group, or a team is able to know what is expected of them as well as the tasks that are assigned to them that make an individual or a specific position in a team relevant.

It helps to avoid confusing situations, avoid conflicts, and establish cooperation. Effective delegation, on the other hand, is characterised by the ability to match people and goal directives, communicate clear, well-understood expectations, provide delegated authority and resources, and open communication channels for progress feedback. It is crucial to understand that when roles are properly defined and tasks delegated, it becomes easy for each team to harness the strengths of the individual members in a bid to accomplish the required objectives.

**For example, consider the following fictional scenario:**

Once, in the city of Pune, there was an IT-based company known as Tech-Innovations. This company was renowned for its new innovative technology and for being able to develop the most effective and efficient mobile applications. However, the teams at Tech-Innovations hinted at some problems in the definition of roles as well as efficiency when it comes to developing an application out of a request from a client.

Suresh, the CEO of this organization, realised that these concerns needed to be resolved and proceeded to act upon them. To address these issues, he decided to convene a meeting with the leadership team in an effort to identify what could be done to enhance role definition and distribution in the organization. In an effort to effectively rectify the issue of role clarity in his organization, Suresh and his leadership team had to consider the best ways of achieving clear roles for every member.

To help clarify their roles and responsibilities, they agreed to compose a document known as the "Roles and Responsibilities Framework." The framework described the duties, responsibilities, and contributions of each role in the organization. They started implementing this framework by focusing on having one-on-one sessions with all the employees in that team.

Suresh and his team reviewed the contents of the document, resolved doubts and ambiguities, and permitted the team members to raise questions. The open communication helped the team members understand where everyone was in the big scheme of things and cultivate a wider perspective. Thus, Suresh was able to effectively handle the role clarity issue for his organization, and it was time for any effective delegation.

When it came to the next topic, which was delegation, Suresh had a story to tell his leadership team. He went head-to-head and shared an instance where he felt most burdened by tasks and duties. His mentor had to come in and show him that he needed to learn how to delegate. Suresh decided to emphasize that the key to the success of the enterprise is in selecting the right man for the job. He agreed to tell the story of how his mentor defined the strengths of employees and how he scheduled work. This not only improved the fun element in the work within each of the teams but also the productivity and morale of each of the teams involved.

From this point of view, the leadership team recommended how among them they could divide the duties for their subgroups. They emphasized clarity of instructions, clear and achievable goals and objectives, and appropriate supervision. From the discussion, the team agreed that other people within the organization should be let to advance professionally by assigning them more tasks to handle. A couple of months later, there were changes at Tech-Innovations.

Once the Roles and Responsibilities Framework was put in place, the teams were more open to sharing information within the organization. To avoid misunderstandings and to provide clearer communication and cooperation between the team members, each of the coming actions was known to the individual team members. In this case, the delegation of work was done effectively, thereby ensuring that the workload was distributed evenly. Team members appeared to be empowered and appreciated as more responsibilities were assigned to them based on their abilities. Its projects began to work in a more coordinated way.

The productivity increased, and the work was accomplished within the time frame as required. Therefore, clients became satisfied with the services being offered, resulting in repeat business and referrals. This short and fictional example shows why it is critical to have clear roles within a team and to delegate tasks correctly.

Now, let's move on to how you can achieve these strategies in your teams. Here are some steps and strategies to achieve role clarity and delegate effectively within teams:

## Role Clarity in Just 5 Simple Steps

I. **Clearly define roles and responsibilities:**

First of all, establish exactly how each person will be involved in the team and what he or she will be doing. Ensure that everyone clearly understands expectations and the impact made by each individual's efforts on the collective goal.

II. **Align with Skills and Interests:**

Minimize conflicts by ensuring as much as possible that workers' skills, aptitudes, and preferences can be well aligned with those roles they are obliged to fill. This promotes commitment and productivity, as people work best when engaged and promoted in areas of interest.

III. **Communicate Expectations:**

Share with the employees the set performance standards, specific goals, and desired behavioral patterns. Be specific on objectives and what is expected to be achieved within a given period, quality to be attained, and criteria that would be used to determine if the goal has been met.

IV. **Avoid Overlapping Roles:**

Prevent role confusion by ensuring that roles are distinct and do not overlap. Clearly define boundaries to prevent conflicts or duplicated efforts.

V. **Regularly Review and Adjust:**

Roles may need to evolve as the team's objectives change. Regularly review and adjust roles to match the team's needs and individual growth.

## Effective Delegation in Just 5 Simple Steps

### 1) Select the Right Person:

Another aspect to consider and work for is the delegation of duties, where assignments should be given according to the member's ability, experience, and the kind of growth he or she would wish to achieve. Consider their capacity and workload before delegating new responsibilities.

**2) Set Clear Expectations:**

When you delegate a task, you should ensure that you give a clear direction, scope of the project, expected results, timelines, and any restrictions. Make it clear to the individual why such a task is crucial in the process.

**3) Provide Authority and Resources:**

Granting authority and resources allows teams to make decisions in alignment with their expertise to complete the task successfully, Lack of authority can hinder progress and decision-making.

**4) Nurture empowerment:**

Give individuals the freedom to approach tasks in their own way. Avoid micromanaging, but be available for guidance and support.

**5) Establish Check- Points:**

To maintain the result-oriented work, arrange the checkpoints of the communication so that they would not only be positive but useful in solving possible complications. This makes it possible to monitor the task and its development and, if need be, make changes.

It is important to understand that role clarity and delegation are not one-time exercises where all the work is done upfront but rather ongoing processes. One must be familiar with the concept of reassessing communication and incorporating means of feedback and flexibility to guarantee that the members of the team stay motivated and productive for the benefit of the team.

## Ensuring Accountability in Delegation

Promoting accountability in delegation simply implies exposing everyone to bear the consequence of any task or responsibility delegated to him or her. It is about ensuring that they know what has to be done and why and that they don't renege on their promises. Accountability means getting done the tasks assigned within a specific time; it means being answerable for the results, good or bad. It is akin to assigning responsibilities and accepting not only their performance of the duty but their awareness of consequences as well. This assists in making people in a certain team or group take charge of what has been provided to them as their task and make sure that goals and objectives are achieved.

**Well, here is what I have come up with for the following assignment for you and your team, which is specifically for role clarification and for delegation.**

**Exercise:** Team Task Shuffle

**Objective**: To measure the extent of role clarity and the level of delegation by swapping over the positions of the team members.

**Instructions:**

- **Role Assignment**: Communicate a different task for each person on the team. These could be positions that they are already acquainted with in the group or those that they will invent for the drill.
- **Task Explanation**: Tell your team to think of a menial activity or a small project that the team can work on together, such as organizing a virtual event
- **Role Shuffle**: Now, ask everyone to swap their roles with a teammate. Each team member will take on the role of another person.
- **Task Execution**: With the new roles, work together to complete the task. The key is to do the task using the roles you've switched to.
- **Debriefing**: On completion of a task, a meeting with the whole team, especially for the purpose of dissection of what has transpired, is a must. How effective was the task going with the changed roles? Was the situation confusing or clear? Were people at ease with their new positions?
- **Learning Points**: Summarize the key learning from the exercise and how it relates to role definition and delegation of duties. What do you discover from each other concerning the roles each of you has displayed?

**Benefits:**

- Offers a hands-on way to experience different roles.
- Tests understanding of roles and effective delegation.
- Encourages learning from each other's perspectives.

Remember, the exercise is meant to be insightful and not evaluative. It's a chance to explore how well roles are understood and how effectively tasks are delegated within your team.

I trust that you've completed this exercise with your team! If Not, I encourage everyone in your team to attempt this activity!

*"The art of effective delegation is not in doing tasks, but in finding the right people to do them."*

***David J. Greer***

**Let's take a moment to ask ourselves the following questions and answer it Honestly :**

1. Has each team member had their task or duty laid down clearly and effectively?

   **(YES / NO)**

   ______________________________________________

   ______________________________________________

2. Are the organizational roles of individual team members clear, and do they comprehend how they link with the work and objectives of the team?

   **(YES / NO)**

   ______________________________________________

   ______________________________________________

3. Am I fairly delegating tasks based on each team member's strength and expertise

   **(YES / NO)**

   ______________________________________________

   ______________________________________________

4. Have I provided clear instructions, expectations, and goals when delegating tasks?

   **(YES / NO)**

   ______________________________________________

   ______________________________________________

Reflecting on the questions mentioned above will help you identify the aspects of role clarity and effective delegation that can produce several advantages regarding the improvement of teamwork, performance, and goals.

Therefore, one can comprehensively agree with the notion that role clarity and delegation are two of the cornerstones that make teams highly functional. The power boost that comes with people understanding the specific roles assigned to them and distributing tasks appropriately comes with many advantages.

These ideas help to prevent confusion and make things easier. Delegation also enables everyone in the team to demonstrate their versatility and support in incredible manners. Besides, when there is a clear understanding of roles and responsibilities and an efficient delegation process, communication improves and people become productive and satisfied.

So, just remember: clearly defined responsibilities, proper assignment of tasks, and your team will achieve incredible results!

As we finish this chapter, get excited for what's coming next: **"Lead by Example."** In the next segment, you will discover the significance of being a great leader. You will learn how your efforts can assist like-minded people to succeed as well. Just imagine how amazing it feels to read real-life cases and practical tips and evidence of how it works when a leader leads by example. Flip the page and learn more on how to transform and become an incredible leader that followers not only obey and replicate but also believe.

# SECRET 03

# LEAD BY AN EXAMPLE

" Leading by example is essential for building an effective team. To create a great team, the leader should set a good example by doing things right. The leader's responsibility, hard work, and commitment demonstrate to the team how they should act as well. This makes everyone accountable and proficient in their work. When the leader leads by actions and not just words, it helps in building trust, teamwork, and a shared goal to succeed. This leads to a team that works well together, achieves success, and gets things done efficiently.

In essence, A leader who sets a good example not only helps the team succeed but also inspires team members to become leaders themselves. This creates a positive legacy of influence that lasts.

*"Lead by example. If you want your team to be punctual, show up on time. If you want them to work hard, you work harder. Your actions should speak louder than words." - **Unknown***

## Modeling the Behaviour You Expect

Once, there was a manufacturing company that was thriving, and the CEO of the company was named Kabir. Kabir was perceived as a boss who had high demands on his subordinates. Nonetheless, while the company was doing well financially, there was discontent over the organizational climate among the employees, and they were not very satisfied.

One day, Kabir decided to do something surprising. He did not hold a regular meeting but informed all the participants that for the next month he would go to different departments of the company to see what they do and how it could be done better. In the first week, Kabir was assigned to work with the customer support department. He was answering phone calls, handling customers' issues, and sometimes working overtime to complete additional tasks.

This made him come to the realization that the team was under a lot of pressure and that they needed better tools to do their work effectively. For the next few weeks, Kabir was placed in other areas of the firm, including production, marketing, and finance.

Thus, he learned what each job was like and tried to find ways to make things better by working more hours. He even requested that the employees give their input and feedback.

As the month progressed, something incredible transpired. Thus, the employees were happier, and the atmosphere in the workplace changed to be more warm and communicative. Everyone was happy that Kabir was with them and was ready to change for the best of the company.

Kabir didn't stop there. He implemented several ideas from the employees, such as getting better software for customer support and keeping work processes easy. This made the company efficient and the employees more satisfied.

In the long run, the transformation occurred, and the company evolved into an environment in which individuals felt like they were all in it together like one large team. The company became more successful, and that is why many talented people wanted to work there.

Kabir's decision to lead by example and work closely with employees made a big difference. It not only fixed the problems in the company but also made the company stronger in the market.

This story shows that even top leaders can make their companies better by understanding their employees and making positive changes based on that understanding. Here are the key takeaways from the story.

- **Lead by Doing**: Kabir showed how leaders should lead not just by saying things but by doing them. He worked alongside his employees to understand their jobs better.
- **Talk and Listen**: Kabir talked to his employees and listened to their ideas and concerns. This made the workplace more open and friendly.
- **Solve Problems Together**: Instead of just finding problems, Kabir worked with his team to find solutions. He made changes based on what the employees suggested, like getting better software and making work easier.
- **Make Work Fun**: Kabir's approach made the employees happier. The workplace became a fun and friendly team, and everyone felt like they were working together for the same goal.
- **Improve and Succeed**: Kabir didn't just fix problems; he made the whole company better. This not only made the employees happier but also helped the company succeed more in the market.
- **Bring in the Best People**: Because Kabir made the company a great place to work, talented people

wanted to join. This shows how a good leader and a positive workplace can attract the best people.

*"Your attitude determines your direction."*

*****John C. Maxwell*****

## Building a Culture of Excellence with Just 7 Strategies

If you want to be successful in leading by example, **here are 7 strategies you should use:**

I. **Honesty:** Be honest and always do the right thing. Show your team that they can trust you and that you have strong values. Be someone they can look up to.

II. **Effective Communication**: Be clear and concise when talking to your team members, be open, and never use harsh words when speaking to your team. Get everyone to speak their minds, usually in a discussion with one's team, and respond accordingly and give feedback.

III. **Work Ethic**: Be punctual, work harder when needed, and be extremely professional in order to set the best example. It also indicates that you take responsibilities seriously

IV. **Accountability**: Accept responsibility for yourself and your actions and be able to accept when you are wrong. This has a way of leading to the development of accountability since the leader is accountable in order to foster the same within the team.

V. **Setting High Standards**: Set standards that define the level of acceptable quality, performance, and standards of conduct. The other is to define the correct regulatory pattern on how activities within the organization should be performed effectively. Also, adhere to those rules and standards and ensure that your team, colleagues, and other staff members do the same.

VI. **Positive Attitude**: Keep a positive attitude no matter the worst situations that may arise. This is important because it was discovered that the manner in which one undertook one's work could either energize or demoralize the whole team.

VII. **Recognition and Appreciation**: Acknowledge the efforts that the people of the organization or the members of your team employed. Praise will help encourage them to continue to work to the same high standard they have depicted earlier. we will learn more about this in upcoming chapter.

## Inspirational Leadership Stories

This is a story of two best friends; in the following story, One friend rose to success by leading by example while the other struggled in life by not doing the same. In a small town, Avani and Meera, best friends, decided to start their own business ventures for their dreams and plans.

Avani started a clothing and fashion company, while Meera launched a business focused on skincare and beauty products. They each followed their passions, creating two separate companies.

In Avani's company, she didn't work closely with her team. She stayed in her fancy office and simply told people what to do. When problems arose, she gave orders but didn't help out. She rarely praised her team's efforts.

Over time, Avani's employees felt unhappy and unappreciated. Their work suffered, and customers started to complain. Communication was poor, leading to confusion. The company lost customers, damaging its reputation.

On the other hand, Meera's company believed in teamwork. She didn't just talk; she showed her team how to do things and worked alongside them. Meera also valued her team's input, thanking them when they did well, which kept them motivated. At Meera's company, everyone worked together and communicated effectively.

As a result, Meera's company thrived. Customers loved them, and more people wanted to do business with them, leading to increased profits. Employees at Meera's company felt proud because they had a supportive leader who led by example.

In the end, **Avani's company** struggled because she didn't lead by example. In contrast, **Meera's company** succeeded, thanks to her leadership style.

From this story, we learn some important lessons:

- **Lead by Doing, Not Just Talking**: The story emphasizes the importance of engaging and working with the team instead of shouting and giving orders to them, as Meera did rather than like Avani, who just gave orders to her team.
- **Appreciate Your Team**: Meera appreciated and acknowledged her team, and this made them have a joyful spirit, which in turn benefited her company. Avani's lack of recognition led to unhappiness and challenges in her company.
- **Communication is Key**: Meera's emphasis on open communication and teamwork created a clear and efficient work environment. Avani's lack of communication resulted in confusion and a decline in her company's performance.
- **Success Comes from Teamwork**: The story highlights that a company's success is closely tied to teamwork. Meera's company thrived because everyone worked together, whereas Avani's company faced challenges due to a lack of collaboration.

- **Leadership Matters**: Meera's leadership style, leading by example, had a positive impact on her company's success, happiness, and reputation. Avani's lack of leadership affected her company negatively.
- **Inspire Others**: The overall message is to inspire others by leading with a positive example. The story is for businesspeople to work on creating organizations that help transform people for the better, an excellent reason to be a good leader.
- Time to lead by example and build a successful and inspiring business.

**Take a moment to ask the following questions:**

1. Do you show honesty and strong ethics through your actions with the team?

   ______________________________________________

   ______________________________________________

2. Do I always maintain a high standard in my work and behaviour?

   ______________________________________________

   ______________________________________________

3. Do I see and praise my team's hard work and success?

   ______________________________________________

   ______________________________________________

4. Do I own up to what I do and decide, or do I leave it to my team?

   ______________________________________________

   ______________________________________________

These questions about leading by example are like asking yourself to look in a mirror to see how you have to change or get better. It helps to identify self and organizational skills, practice and use interpersonal communication, and undertake the tasks required.

If this can be done regularly, then it will go a long way to building trust and a productive workforce in the particular team, while on the other hand the members of the team will be much happier. It is like sowing seeds for future gains and making sure that the working environment is nice.

Therefore, getting people to emulate your actions should be considered one of the most effective motivation strategies since you lead by example instead of using words. Thus, trust is also developed together with a good tone in the organization or company.

It also increases the sense of belongingness, and therefore there is a positive change in the quality of communication that makes organizations more joyful and productive. It is a leadership style that has the potential to influence the lives of individuals and the world, making it worth having people in society.

As we conclude this chapter on leading by example, it's important to get excited about the next one: **"Management of Conflict"** There is always conflict in any group; that's how it is, but how they are resolved is very important. In the next part, you will find out how different people can manage their conflicts and solve the issues that they have peacefully. So, get ready! Now, let's discover how to work on our team by learning best practices when it comes to managing conflicts.

# SECRET 04

# MANAGEMENT OF CONFLICT

"Managing conflict constructively within teams is important for creating a good and productive work environment. When in your team if something like a fight or argument happens, it has to be handled well. This means communicating and interacting with each other politely and without biases, not involving severeness or anger.

Teams should also have clear rules for solving these problems. This way, the team can work together to find solutions and make things better. Conflict, when handled well, can lead to new ideas and better teamwork. So, teams that manage conflicts nicely can do their jobs better and get along well with each other.

## Conflict in the Workplace

The following is a story of a team of workers in a spirited organization in Mumbai.

Once upon a time, there was a project in the organization. All the team members had diverse working experiences and knowledge, and they all introduced their thinking to the work. Nevertheless, it has to be observed that as the project unfolded, conflicts also started to happen. One day, as the deadline approached, two team members, Raj and Priya, found themselves at odds over the project's direction.

Raj believed in a traditional approach, while Priya thought a more innovative approach was needed. Their disagreements became increasingly heated, and it began to affect the overall team morale.

Recognizing the need to address the conflict constructively, their boss, Aisha, called a meeting. Aisha said it's okay to have different ideas because it can help make things better. She asked Raj and Priya to explain their ideas, and other team members also shared their thoughts.

During the meeting, Aisha encouraged Raj and Priya to share their perspectives openly. Raj then moved on, saying that it is best to remain conservative and do things the traditional way since previous projects have been finished this way. While on the side of Priya, she pointed out the fast-evolving market conditions and the necessity to introduce some change in the business model.

Aisha followed the arguments of both parties patiently and then introduced the suggestions of the team. Other team members shared their thoughts, offering a middle-ground solution that incorporated elements of both Raj and Priya's ideas. Aisha also appreciated the work done by both the design and the development teams and proposed conducting a pilot project to use this approach.

In the next few weeks, the team would be collaborating on the pilot project, and what they produced was the pilot project. Not only did it help to bring together the best of both the traditional and the innovative, but also the team was more unified. Raj and Priya worked at understanding each other's views and started working in unison.

Finally, the project was done successfully at the agreed time and much to the pleasure of the client. Let alone, the conflict was solved by the team and made them even more united. They also found out that it is advantageous to deal with conflict in a positive way because this forms positive results and encourages group unity, and this they took with them from the project.

This team's story serves as a reminder that diversity of thought when managed with respect and collaboration, can lead to innovation and success.

So here are some takeaways that you can implement in your office

- **Different Ideas Are Good**: The team had people with different backgrounds and ideas. Having varied perspectives is helpful because it brings more creative solutions.
- **Talk About Problems**: Instead of fighting, the boss, Aisha, gathered everyone to talk about the issues. This is important to solve problems and make things better.

- **Share Your Thoughts**: Aisha made a space for everyone to share what they think. This helped in finding solutions and understanding each other better.
- **Use Both Old and New Ideas**: The team found success by using a bit of both old and new ideas. It's like mixing what worked before with some new ways to get the best results.
- **Work Together to Solve Issues**: Aisha asked everyone for ideas to solve the problem. This teamwork helped in finding a solution that everyone liked.
- **Try Out New Ideas First**: Before doing something big, like the whole project, the team tested a small part first. This way, they could see if the new idea was good before using it for everything.
- **Get Closer as a Team**: Solving problems together made the team stronger and closer. It's like becoming better friends while working together.
- **Learn from Problems**: The team learned that when there are problems, talking and working together can make things better. They decided to use this lesson for their future projects to make them even more successful.

*"The best way to solve problems and to fight against war is through dialogue."*

*****Malala Yousafzai*****

## 7 Techniques for Resolving Conflict

Now, it is time to look at the 7 methods that we are able to utilize in order to manage and solve conflicts in the teams.

I. **Talk to Each Other**: In case there is a problem, the members of the team should engage in a discussion and try to listen to one another. No interrupting, just listening.

II. **Follow the Rules**: Have a clear plan for solving problems. Ensure that all the people know what to do when there is a problem.

III. **Get Help if Needed**: If the problem is too complex, it is advisable to call an unbiased person who can give an answer, for example, a manager or a mediator.

IV. **Work Together**: Don't get involved in conflict; instead, try to resolve it. Always think about the good of others and not only your own good.

V. **Talk Regularly**: Keep having team meetings where everyone can say how they feel. It stops problems from getting worse and makes everyone feel heard.

VI. **Put Yourself in Their Shoes**: Try to see things through another person or your team's eyes, or at least how he or she might feel about it. It helps you get along better.

VII. **Learn from Problems**: After a fight is over, think about what happened and how to avoid it next time. It's like learning from mistakes, so things get better in the future.

VIII. **Learn from Problems**: After a fight is over, think about what happened and how to avoid it next time. It's like learning from mistakes, so things get better in the future.

*"The aim of argument or of discussion should not be victory, but progress."*

***Joseph Joubert***

## Making a Positive Place to Solve Problems.

Establishing the climate for problem-solving and handling conflicts is like preparing a comfortable nest where all people will solve problems with pleasure. It's not just about being courteous; it's about being expressive and communicating well when things do not pan out as planned.

The main emphasis is placed on finding solutions and improving situations instead of blaming people for mistakes that occurred. In this happy environment, people assume that they are members of a productive team that cooperates with their fellow team members. So, it is like transforming challenges into a process of strengthening and developing the relationship.

In this inspiring environment, not only do employees cooperate effectively, but they are also motivated to assist the group in realizing its objectives. This positive approach then forms one of the crucial foundations for continuous success and a happy, integrated team.

**So here is an assignment for you and your team for conflict resolution.**

**Assignment Title:** Conflict Resolution and Management Exercise

**Objective:** To help the teams strengthen their problem-solving skills when there is conflict.

**Instructions:**

- **Team Formation**: Divide into groups of 4-6 individuals and ensure that the groups have people with different kinds of skills and expertise.
- **Conflict Scenario**: Provide each team with an issue that never occurred, but they have to 'face,' such as how to complete a given assignment or what to do when two employees are not on the same page.
- **Think About It**: When you worked in a group, discuss the ways where the issue occurred and ways where all the group members contributed to worsening the problem.
- **Make a Plan**: Discuss with one another and determine how the problem will be resolved. Decide how you are going to communicate with each other and what steps will have to be taken to resolve the conflict.
- **Act It Out**: Act like you are those people in the problem and solve it with the help of your plan. Make it like a play.

- **Talk About It**: When you are done, you should discuss the strengths you had while exercising as well as the areas of improvement next time.
- **Help Each Other**: Always advise other groups on how they could improve on their problem-solving abilities.
- **Write About It**: Each person should write a short story about what they learned and how they can use it in real life.
- **Show and Tell**: Explain to the whole class what you did and the lesson learned as well.

**Benefits of this exercise?**

The "Conflict Resolution and Management Exercise" assignment has some important benefits.

- It helps you learn how to deal with problems and arguments better, which is useful in your personal and work life.
- It also makes you better at talking to people and understanding their feelings. You get better at understanding yourself too.
- You learn how to stop conflicts from happening in the first place.
- It makes you work better with others, which is good for getting things done and making everyone happy.

**Before moving forward** "Have you completed the previous assignment with your team?" The conflict handling assignment is an opportunity to learn how to communicate and deal with issues concerning people. It's like learning a super handy trick that may prove useful both in the workplace and when dealing with friends. Don't wait; try and do your best, and most importantly, this assignment will make the whole team work better.

**Take a moment to ask the following questions?**

1. Do I listen well when I'm in a conflict?

   ______________________________________________

   ______________________________________________

   Do I get angry easily, or do I stay polite even when in conflict?

   ______________________________________________

   ______________________________________________

   Have I been involved in the conflict, and if so, how much?

   ______________________________________________

   ______________________________________________

2. Am I good at working with other people to find solutions?

   ______________________________________________

   ______________________________________________

So, if you answer these questions very honestly, you can come with ways for improving interpersonal conflict management in the team and, also, the overall team performance.

Now, as we finish this chapter on handling conflicts in teams, let's move to the next part: **'Accountability and Measurement'**. This part of our journey will involve a mandate of specific duties, goal setting, and feedback.

Similar to having good ways of solving conflict, these things are essential in order to ensure that we are giving our best shot. Therefore, let us look forward to the things that we will study in the next chapter in order to improve on team performance and achievements.

# # SECRET 05

# ACCOUNTABILITY AND MEASUREMENT

"Accountability and measurement are like the GPS and fuel gauge for teams. They provide accountability—teams have a clear understanding of where they are headed while measurement shows them how well they are likely to perform this. This is super important because it peruses the course of work of the team and aids in shaping it and correcting or future-proofing it. The following is our discussion of why those things are important and how they can be used on teams to achieve goals.

Try to think about a soccer game where goals are not displayed on the field or a map with no Landmarks, it just won't make sense and people will hardly have an idea whether they are winning or losing. Similarly, teams require methods or ways of being held accountable and benchmarks that will help them in a process of correcting themselves to higher levels of performance or in achieving these predefined objectives.

In today's topic, we will explore the effectiveness of using accountability and measurement concepts within teams. Imagine a bustling city like Bangalore, where a graphic design company named 'Pixel Perfection' faced a common challenge which was achieving client's delivery requirements in coordination with delivering the best quality services. Thus, with the leadership of their founder, Maya, the team started a process of design improvement through the application of accountability and measurement strategies.

Maya decided it was time to introduce accountability and measurement to enhance their design process. She gathered her team and implemented a new approach.

First, Maya assigned each designer specific projects based on their strengths and interests. By this, everyone knew what they had to do and felt more responsible for their work. She also started a system where each designer would check a teammate's work before it was sent to the client.

To measure progress, Maya introduced a project tracking software where designers could update their project status daily. They could mark tasks as "In Progress," "Completed," or "Needs Review." This helped everyone stay on the same page and reduced last-minute rushes.

As a final touch, Maya established a monthly team meeting called "Design Showcase." During these meetings, designers would present their completed projects, discuss challenges they faced, and share feedback and ideas for improvement.

Over time, Pixel Perfection experienced a remarkable transformation. Accountability made designers more responsible for their projects, and the quality control system ensured that every design was top-notch. The project tracking software helped them meet deadlines consistently, and the Design Showcase meetings encouraged collaboration and continuous improvement.

Pixel Perfection's reputation soared, and they began receiving more clients and projects. Maya's approach of introducing accountability and measurement not only enhanced the quality of their work but also strengthened the team's unity and creativity.

This shows how accountability (clear roles and quality control) and measurement (project tracking and team meetings) can significantly boost a creative team's productivity and reputation, ultimately leading to their success.

Let's break down the important lessons from the story into simpler terms:

- **Everyone Has a Job**: Maya gave each designer specific projects based on what they are good at. This way, everyone knew exactly what they were responsible for.
- **Check Each Other's Work**: Maya made sure that before a design went to the client, another designer would look at it to make sure it was really good. This helped in making sure every design was excellent.
- **Use a Special Computer Program**: Maya introduced a special computer program where designers could update what they were working on every day. This helped them stay organized, finish things on time, and avoid last-minute stress.

- **Talk About Work Together**: Maya started a monthly meeting where designers could show their finished projects, talk about any problems they faced, and share ideas on how to do better. This made the team work well together.
- **Be Responsible**: Making everyone responsible for their work made the designs even better. This meant that each person took their job seriously.
- **Get Better Together**: The changes Maya made not only made the designs better but also made the team stronger. They became so good that more clients wanted them to do projects.
- **Always Try to Improve**: The story shows that even when things are going well, there's always a way to do even better. Talking about problems and sharing ideas helps the team keep improving.

*"What gets measured gets managed."*

*****Peter Drucker*****

## Key Performance Indicators (KPIs)

Let's identify how you can use these indicators with your team. By implementing these key steps, you can pave the way for your team's accountability and measurement.

I. **Clearly Assign Jobs:** Make sure everyone knows what their job is, so nobody is confused.

II. **Set Clear Goals**: Have specific targets everyone can understand.

III. **Keep an Eye on Progress**: Regularly check how things are going to catch problems early.

IV. **Use Important Numbers:** Find and use numbers that show how well the team is doing.

V. **Hold People Responsible**: Make sure everyone does their part and reward those who do well.

VI. **Talk Openly:** Encourage everyone to talk and share problems or ideas.

VII. **Learn and Improve:** Keep looking at how the team is doing and make changes to make it better.

In this **7 Secrets Of Effortless Team Success,** "Accountability and Measurement" is the secret which is the map that directs teams toward their objectives. Realising roles and goals, control of the process, use of key performance indicators, individual responsibility, teamwork, free exchange of information, and process optimization can facilitate employee and team success, well-being, and efficiency. Implementing these strategies creates a plan for not only achieving goals but surpassing them and setting the foundation for long-term success and progression for oneself and the entire team.

It is crucial to ensure that you incorporate these strategies since applying them is like having a blueprint to follow as a team. When you follow these steps, you know who should do what, where you are headed, and whether you will achieve goals along the way. It is like a plan where you work and achieve success side by side!

*"Accountability breeds response-ability." -*

*****Stephen R. Covey*****

## Holding Teams Accountable

In the textile town of Coimbatore, there was a small weaving firm called "WeaveUnity." This firm had skilled weavers who made nice and beautiful handwoven fabrics. However, they faced a common problem keeping up with consistent quality and production schedules.

Leading the firm was Anika, who believed that accountability and measurement could solve these challenges. She introduced the following practices:

1. **Clear Role Assignments**: Anika assigned specific roles to each weaver based on their expertise, ensuring that

everyone knew their responsibilities in the weaving process.

2. **Quality Standards**: She established clear quality standards for the fabrics, defining what constituted a top-notch product. These standards included factors like thread count, color consistency, and finish.

3. **Production Targets**: Anika set achievable daily production targets for each team member, providing clear guidelines for their work.

4. **Regular Quality Checks**: The firm implemented a system of regular quality checks throughout the weaving process. Weavers checked each other's work to keep high standards.

5. **Accountability Meetings**: They had weekly meetings to talk about progress, fix problems, and share ideas on how to improve their weaving skills.

Over time, Weave Unity's fabrics were praised for their excellent quality and on-time delivery. Their products became very popular, not just in local markets but also around the world. Anika's focus on responsibility and measuring results made the cooperative's products better and more efficient. It also built a stronger sense of pride and teamwork among the weavers.

This story from Coimbatore shows how adding responsibility and measurement can improve a team's performance and reputation, even in traditional industries like weaving.

## Tracking Progress and Performance

In the business world, it is the same as tracking how well the company is doing by evaluating its progress and performance. In organizations, managers establish objectives, which might be called goals, and then they always monitor how far off they are from attaining them.

They do this by using tools called Key Performance Indicators (KPIs), which help them monitor their work in different areas, including sales, customer satisfaction, and the time taken to complete projects.

These KPIs serve as flags that show if the business is heading in the right direction. If things are not as expected, tracking progress helps businesses make changes as soon as possible. It is like a ship sailing on water; if it is off course, one wants to know so that one can alter direction.

All this encourages everyone in the business to perform optimally and constantly seek better ways for the firm to be productive and relevant in the market.

**So Here Is An Assignment For You And Your Team To Monitor Accountability And Measurement!**

**Assignment Title:** Team Goal Tracking Challenge

**Objective:** The objective of this assignment is to introduce and practice accountability and measurement in a team setting by tracking and achieving team goals.

**Assignment Description:**

- **Team Formation:** Gather teams of 3-4 members. In this activity, Each team will choose a common goal they want to achieve within a specific time span. It should be a goal that is connected to the team's interests, and it can be as basic as a fitness challenge, a charity drive, or achieving a set number of goals personally or at the workplace.
- **Goal Definition:** Each team member should clearly define their selected goal. They should describe what success looks like, specify the deadline for achieving that goal and accordingly assign responsibilities within the team
- **Measurement Metrics:** Teams should identify important metrics or indicators that will help measure progress toward the goal. For instance, if the intended goal is a fitness challenge, metrics might include the number of workouts done, weight loss, or distance covered.

- **Weekly Updates:** During the duration of the assignment, different teams will provide weekly feedback to the instructor or team members. Some of these updates should include a summary of progress made, any challenges encountered, and actions taken to overcome them.
- **Peer Accountability:** Every Team member should hold each other accountable for their contributions towards the goal. They can use a simple accountability system, such as daily check-ins or a shared progress document.
- **Final Presentation:** So at the end of the entire assignment, each team will give a brief presentation to the group. They should share and describe their experiences, what metrics they used to track progress, and whether or not they accomplished their goal.
- **Reflection:** After completing the assignment, team members should discuss what worked well, what didn't, and what they learned about the importance of accountability and measurement in achieving their goals.
- **Grading Criteria:** The assessment of teams will be evaluated based on their goal definition, regular reports, the extent to which they achieved their goal, and the quality of their final presentation and reflection that follows.

**Benefits:**

This assignment is very helpful in teaching accountability and measurement concepts, especially to people who have never worked in groups or teams before. It stresses goal definition, monitoring with the provision of appropriate tools for evaluating the team's performance, and ensuring team members are responsive. It will also enable the team to learn how these principles could be used to attain both individual and group targets.

Overall, this assignment can be considered a rather easy yet highly efficient method to explain the concepts of accountability and measurement within a team environment. It particularly focuses on goal orientation, defining measurable targets, and ensuring the team's members are held responsible for their work outputs. The team will also understand how the mentioned principles can be used to accomplish personal and team goals.

I'd like to motivate you and say, "Yes, do it!" This is more like a fun game where both you and your team develop goals, learn how to achieve them, and then see the outcome. This can help you learn how keeping track of what you do can help you reach your goals in any activity. You can do it! I'll be with you every step! Please worry not and try your best!

**Let's Hold for a moment and Engage yourself In Some Self-Reflection Questions:**

1. Which are my Specific Goals and their Objectives?

   ______________________________________________

   ______________________________________________

2. Do I always measure the Progress of these Goals and Objectives, if yes how?

   ______________________________________________

   ______________________________________________

3. What problems did I face during my goals achievement, and how did I handle them?

   ______________________________________________

   ______________________________________________

So, use these principles and watch your team reach new heights! As we finish talking about how to make teams accountable and measure their progress, let's get excited about the next chapter: "**Empower and Trust**. It's like turning the page to a new adventure in our teamwork journey. means letting each team member have the freedom and responsibility to do their best, like giving them special powers. Trust is always like a glue that holds the team together, and making sure everyone works well with each other. In the upcoming chapter, we'll learn how these two things can help teams achieve amazing things. So, get ready to explore how to make your team even more awesome!

# SECRET 06

# EMPOWER AND TRUST

"In our workplace, we support our team by providing them with the right tools and help to do their best work. This is called empowerment. When people feel empowered, they feel more confident and motivated to face challenges. Trust is important for empowerment—it means we rely on each other and value everyone's efforts. By creating a workplace with empowerment and trust, we help everyone work better together and reach their full potential.

*"Empowerment is not giving people power, but releasing the power they already have."*

***John Stahl-Wert***

## Encouraging Independence in the Workplace.

There was a team of workers in a corporate office who once had a day in a week known as 'Self-Organizing Team Day.' On this day, the boss of the company, Mr. Murty, allowed the workers to work independently without supervising them.

During Self-Organizing Team Day, Mr. Murty assembled the group and exclaimed, "Today is a remarkable day. I have the utmost confidence in you to work, to decide, and to solve problems without specific direction from me. You are full of potential, and I believe in every one of you."

Initially, the team members felt a little stressed because they had not been engaged in a project without the direct supervision of Mr. Murty. However, as the day progressed, the employees began to cooperate. They defined what they each had to do and, in the process, formulated their strategies and objectives.

During the day, the team had some difficulties, such as group members' schedule conflicts or various unexpected difficulties. However, they didn't panic. They discussed it and came up with solutions on their own. In particular, they found new methods for optimizing their performance and being helpful to each other.

At the end of the Self-Organizing Team Day, the team had completed all their activities and even worked more effectively than on regular days. Mr. Murty was indeed elated and proud to be associated with the kind of accomplishments that his team had made.

He called them again together and said, "Today is proof that when you are given the choice to self-organize and collaborate, you can achieve many great things. So from now on, I expect you to fend for yourselves again; you are a team of empowered individuals capable of making decisions and solving problems on your own."

From that day on, the team felt more confident and motivated. They knew they could rely on each other and make important decisions together. Self-Organizing Team

Day had shown them the power of empowerment, trust, and teamwork in the office, and they continued to thrive as a strong and self-organizing team.

Empowering and trusting your team is like giving them the freedom and confidence to do their best work together. It's like saying, "I believe in you, and I know you can make important decisions and contribute your ideas." This is important because it helps the team work better, solve problems, and reach their goals, just like Mr. Murty's story showed us. When people feel trusted and empowered, they are happier and work harder, and this helps the whole team do well. So, it's like the secret sauce for a successful team!

So when are you organizing a "self-organizing team day" in your office? I believe this is the best time to start. Building strong and successful teams means giving them power and trust. Here are five simple ways to help your teams feel trusted and empowered.

## Guiding Employees Toward Success in 5 Simple Steps.

I. **Set Clear Expectations:**

   - Clear roles, responsibilities, and expectations for each team member should be defined.

- Make sure that everyone remembers their individual and collective goals.
- Set clear ways to measure progress and see how things are going.

II. **Empower Through Decision-Making:**

- Let team members be part of decisions making processes, especially those that directly affect their work.
- Encourage group discussions and idea-sharing to generate diverse ideas.
- Let team members make decisions within their areas of expertise.

III. **Supportive Leadership:**

- Lead by example and demonstrate trust in your team members.
- Be accessible and available to provide guidance and support when needed.
- Encourage leadership development within the team, allowing members to take on leadership roles when appropriate or conduct "Self-Organizing Team Day".

IV. **Conflict Resolution and Collaboration:**

- Create a framework to handle conflicts in a positive way.

- Encourage open talks when disagreements arise, and promote a culture of understanding and compromise.
- Support teamwork by showing the value of different ideas and skills.

V. **Appreciate Differences and Make Everyone Feel Welcome:**

- Create a friendly environment where everyone feels important and heard.
- Welcome and appreciate the differences among your team members, like their unique skills and viewpoints.
- Put in place programs and actions to make sure everyone has an equal chance to participate and succeed in the team."

By using these simple strategies, you can create an environment where team members will feel confident to make decisions, take charge of their work, and trust each other. This in turn can boost team spirit, work output, and overall success. Remember, building trust and confidence in a team requires commitment and dedication from both leaders and team members.

I propose implementing empowerment and trust strategies in our organization. These principles can boost teamwork, creativity, and productivity. Let's discuss how to include them into our daily routine work.

*"Trust is the highest form of human motivation. It brings out the very best in people."*

***Stephen R. Covey***

## Building Trust Among Your Office Team!

- **Get Everyone on Board:** Always make sure everyone in your office understands the importance of trust and empowerment.
- **Talk and Listen:** Always Share ideas and listen when others have something to say.
- **Trust Everyone**: Believe that your coworkers can do their jobs well.

- **Let People Decide**: Give coworkers the freedom to make choices about their work.
- **Help and Be Nice:** Support your coworkers when they need it and be friendly.
- **Say "Good Job":** Tell your coworkers they're doing well when they do.
- **Keep Checking:** Keep an eye on how things are going and make changes if needed.
- **Be a Good Example:** Show your coworkers how to trust and be trusted by doing it yourself.
- **Keep Going**: Building trust and empowerment takes time, so stay committed to these principles, and you'll see positive changes in your office.

**Simple Activity**

Let's do a simple activity to build trust and empowerment in a team:

**Activity**: Team Problem-Solving Challenge

**Objective**: To boost teamwork, decision-making, and trust.

Instructions:

- **Form Teams**: In your office, create teams of 3-5 people. Mix different departments or roles for diversity.

- **Give a challenge**: Give a real or hypothetical problem to each team. The problem could be a work related issue, a creative task, or a fun brain puzzle.
- **Set a time limit**: Allow a set time to each team, like 30 minutes or an hour, to come up with a solution to the challenge.
- **No External Help**: Make sure that the teams should find the solution on their own without seeking advice or help from outside sources
- **Problem-Solving Process**: Encourage teams to talk about the challenge, brainstorm ideas and come up with a solution together.
- **Solution Presentation**: After the time is over, each team explains their solution to the rest of the members in the office. They should be able to demonstrate how they arrived at such a conclusion, and this should be well explained.
- **Feedback and Discussion**: After the time is up, each team presents its solution to the rest of the office.Always they should explain their thought process and how they will reached their conclusion.
- **Reflection**: After that, have a debriefing where team members share what they learned about working together, making right decisions and trusting each other during the activity.

- **Recognition**: Go through all the teams and tell them how good the job is and that the task would not be complete while everyone works alone but as a team believing in each other's capabilities to find solutions.
- **Repeat often:** Also you can make this a repetitive activity to continuously strengthen teamwork and trust within your office.

Doing this activity helps team members to work together, solve problems, make decisions, and trust each other's abilities. It's a simple but best way to promote empowerment and trust in a fun and engaging manner.

Also Completing this activity faster rather than later will not only benefit you but also help you to the collective progress of the team. So let me take you through and make sure you conduct this activity in your organization together!

**"Let's take a moment for self reflection and find the answers and direction we need."**

**Empowerment:**

1) Do team members feel they have liberty to make decisions related to their work?

_______________________________________________

_______________________________________________

2) Are individuals inspire to take ownership of their tasks and projects every time?

_______________________________________________

_______________________________________________

3) Do they think their input is valued and are taken into consideration for important decisions?

_______________________________________________

_______________________________________________

**Trust:**

1) Is there a culture of open and honest discussion with the team?

_______________________________________________

_______________________________________________

2) Do team members believe that their efforts are valued and appreciated here?

_______________________________________________

_______________________________________________

3) Does trust flows both ways from leader to team member?

_______________________________________________

_______________________________________________

Your ideas and opinions matter for making the team better. Please take a moment to answer these above questions. Your answers to this questions will help your team to work more cooperatively and accomplish goals easily. Your input which matters most to empower and trust your team.

As we wind up the topic of empowerment and trust for our team, it is very important to recognize that these are the main two elements of the foundation upon which our collective achievements are built. Empowerment is about giving team members the confidence and power to make decisions and take responsibility, unleashing their maximum potential.

And on the other hand trust is the bond that unites us together, creating an environment where we can openly communicate, collaborate, and innovate. It's because of trust that we nurture a sense of belonging and value each other's contributions. As we move ahead, Let us never forget that empowerment and trust are not equal to slogans alone, but they are the spirits of teams' achievements.

By continuing this way to empower and trust one another, we ensure that our team remains strong, adaptable, and capable of surmounting any challenge that comes our way. It's this commitment to empowerment and trust that will guide us towards a future filled with achievement and joy.

As we come to the end of this chapter on empowerment and trust, let's get excited about what lies ahead in our final chapter: which is **Recognition and Reward**. It's about acknowledging and celebrating our efforts and accomplishments as a team. It is like giving high- five for all team members, which contributes to the transition to new successes! So, get ready for an amazing rewarding finale, as we'll celebrate the victory together!

# SECRET 07

# RECOGNITION AND REWARD

> “Recognizing and rewarding a team means valuing and giving credit to the people who work together. It is like saying, “ I appreciate your efforts “, or ‘Well done,’ or “good job” as a sign that their efforts are recognized and appreciated. This makes every person feel happy and motivated to work, which will increase the performance of team that is being done. It’s like clapping for them or motivating them to keep on doing the good work that they have been doing.

## The Power of Recognition

In a busy office in Bengaluru, a team of customer service representatives worked for a top e-commerce company. Their job was to help customers with their orders, solve any concerns, and make sure every person had a smooth shopping experience.

One day, a particularly challenging situation arose when a high-profile customer faced a complex issue with their order. The team rallied together, putting in extra hours and going above and beyond to find a solution. After diligent effort and collaboration, they managed to resolve the problem to the customer's utmost satisfaction.

Recognizing the exceptional teamwork and dedication displayed, the team leader Bharat knew it was crucial to acknowledge their efforts. In a special meeting, the entire team gathered to celebrate their achievement.

Each team member was called forward and presented with a "Customer Champion" award. This award was based on their problem solving, teamwork, and their orientation to customer needs. With the award, they were also given a gift voucher as a token of appreciation.

They quickly began to approach their tasks with more energy and commitment, and the improved cooperation helped them raise their work to a new level that was admired in the office.

The team felt really happy and close-knit because they knew that working together had a big positive effect. They went back to their desks feeling more determined and confident, ready to handle any problem that came their way.

To make sure everyone kept doing great work, the company started a program to give extra benefits. The best team members got chances to move up in their careers, learn special skills, and even go to important industry events. This way, everyone had even more motivation to do their best!

This combination of recognition and rewards transformed the team's outlook. They became more motivated, proactive, and eager to excel in their roles. Customer satisfaction ratings soared, and the team's reputation for exceptional service spread throughout the company.

This story from the e-commerce office from Bengaluru proves that when you say "good job" and give extra rewards to those who do well, it makes the team work even harder. This makes them do a great job together, and that's a big part of why the company does so well.

*"Appreciation is a wonderful thing. It makes what is excellent in others belong to us as well."*

***Voltaire***

With good recognition and reward practices, employees are encouraged to give their best for organizations and also witness that their teams will deliver well beyond par performances. Moreover, we will explore various reasons why it is important to recognize and reward teams, showcasing their impact on employee engagement, retention, and ultimately, the organization's bottom line.

Here are a few key reasons why it's crucial:

## Simple Reasons Why Recognition Matters:

- **Boosts Morale:** Human beings get a great sense of satisfaction when they feel appreciated in the workplace. This positivity can extend to all members of the team to have a better working environment overall.
- **Increases Productivity:** Appreciation of effort motivates people to continue to give their best effort. When employees are motivated, they always perform their tasks well because they know that whatever they do is appreciated.
- **Nurtures Teamwork**: It reinforces the idea that everyone's contribution is important. It can improve relationships between team members and make them more willing to help each other.
- **Improves Retention**: When people feel recognized and valued, they're more likely to stay with a company. This minimizes and helps to save costs and time that an organization may incur when recruiting and training new employees.

- **Encourages Innovation**: Feeling valued and trusted will create the desire to innovate as well as find new ideas. It ensures that team members are in a position to share their innovative thoughts and suggestions.
- **Enhances Loyalty**: Recognizing and rewarding a team's efforts shows that the company cares about its employees. This creates loyalty and commitment since employees are more likely to stay with a company that appreciates their hard work.
- **Drives Results:** t is widely understood that if a team knows that their work is noticed and valued, they're more likely stretch themselves to go the extra mile to achieve the goals and meet deadlines.
- **Creates a Positive Culture**: Rewarding employees for their work is incredibly important for creating a conducive working environment. It helps everyone appreciate, respect, and support each other.

To summarize, saying thanks and recognizing a team is a great way to encourage and motivate employees. leading to a more productive, satisfied, and successful work environment. It's a win-win for both the employees and the organization.

## Implementing vs. Neglecting Change

In a small village in Rajasthan, there were two brothers, Ram and Shyam who each owned a farm next to each other. They both grew the same crops and faced similar weather challenges.

Ram believed in the power of recognizing the hard work of his farm laborers. He would often take a moment to thank them for their dedication, especially during the harvest season. He introduced a small tradition of offering a meal together as a way of showing gratitude.

Shyam, on the other hand, while a good farmer, didn't prioritize recognition as much. He paid his laborers their wages and expected them to do their jobs without much acknowledgment.

As the seasons changed, a noticeable difference emerged between the two farms. Ram's farm workers felt appreciated and valued. They worked hard and took pride in their work to make sure they had a great harvest. Sharing meals helped them feel close and build a strong community.

On Shyam's farm, the laborers worked diligently but without the same level of enthusiasm. They appreciated the wages but didn't have the same personal connection to the work.

One year, a severe drought hit the region, making farming especially challenging. Both farms struggled, but Ram's workers were determined to overcome the odds. They worked tirelessly, knowing that their efforts were recognized and valued.

On Shyam's farm, the labourer's had the same problems but didn't feel as motivated, so it was harder for them to keep going.

When the monsoon finally came and helped the dry land, the difference was clear. Ram's farm, despite the initial struggles, managed to yield a decent harvest. The labourers, driven by a sense of belonging and recognition, had put in their best effort.

Shyam's farm, though still productive, faced a slightly lower yield. The labourers, though skilled, had faced more difficulty without the same level of acknowledgment.

This story highlights the impact of recognition and appreciation, even in the agricultural setting of a small Indian village. Ram's farm thrived under the culture of appreciation, consistently surpassing expectations. Shyam's farm, while proficient, faced occasional challenges due to the absence of regular acknowledgment.

I understand you might find it unusual to draw a parallel between the story of the farmers Ram and Shyam and the concept of recognition and rewards in an office. However, if we replace the farms with our office space, the labourers with our team, and the difficulties with our challenges, we can see that the solution remains the same. The principle of recognizing and rewarding efforts applies universally, whether in a farm or an office setting."

It serves as a reminder that a little appreciation and recognition can go a long way in motivating and inspiring individuals, just saying "thank you" and recognizing someone's efforts, no matter where you are, can make a big difference.

*"A person who feels appreciated will always do more than what is expected."*

***Unknown***

**Finding Your Best Self:**

**How Looking Inward Can Help?**

1) Can we think of a recent goal we reached together?

______________________________________________

______________________________________________

2) Who on our team deserves a special shout-out for their support?

______________________________________________

______________________________________________

3) How do we want to celebrate our successes as a team?

______________________________________________

______________________________________________

Asking these questions is crucial because when we recognize and reward our team, it's done in a way that really matters to them. It shows that we care about what they think and feel.

This makes the acknowledgment more special and makes everyone feel included. It also keeps communication open and makes the team feel good, which keeps them motivated and happy. So, in simple words, asking these questions makes the recognition and rewards more meaningful and effective for everyone.

# Conclusion

Let me take this opportunity to thank all of you for being a part of 'Effortless Team Success.' As a collective, we have delved into the basics of creating and maintaining optimum-performing teams. From the necessity of clear communication to the wonders of workplace rewards and recognition, every chapter has been enlightening.

Before you put down this book, it is important to ponder the key points presented in it. Try to understand how such important aspects as communication, goal setting, delegation, leadership, conflict, responsibilities, authority, trust, and recognition can lead to the best performance of your team.

However, let me state it clearly: this is not the end but the beginning of something new. Team management is a continuous process, and it is not easy to construct a significant team and lead it effectively.

The possibilities for your team are immense, and by adopting the guidance given in this book, you are in a good position to foster positive change.

As someone once said, "**A team is not a group of people working together; a team is a group of people who trust**

**each other.**" May trust be the foundation of your teams, and may you always lead with passion and principles.

As you begin the process of empowering your team, stay focused on the process; each enhancement is part of the overall transition. Here's to your team: to achieve success and development, to actualize the potential you carry within you. Again, thank you for being a part of this book, and may you and your team triumph and flourish more in the future."

www.ingramcontent.com/pod-product-compliance
Lightning Source LLC
LaVergne TN
LVHW041119150826
845673LV00007B/2122
*9798895888230*